A Post-Capitalist Manifesto

London

May 2010

Published in 2010 by Lulu

ISBN 978-0-557-50141-0

For you

CONTENTS

PART ONE

INTRODUCTIONS

INTRODUCTION

Many people today are yearning for a different way of life. It's no longer just the hippies who want a bit less computer and a bit more earth under the feet and sky over the head; it's also some engineers, policymakers, account managers, financial modelers, cultural entrepreneurs, ethnic minority 'youf', people like me, people like you, perhaps, a little bit of everyone maybe, each in our own way.

THE BLENDED LIFESTYLE

I like my work. It involves laptops and meetings and typing fast and diagrams and ideas and imagining things and finding out about things and trying to make things happen.

I call this work 'trade'. I'm writing this from my favourite café in Berkeley, California, where years ago I used to pore over political science texts and essays. For years and years, formally and informally, I've been developing a set of skills that I trade for money. I use that money to meet some of my needs. I call this 'trade'.

I don't want to do this work five days a week. I'd like more time in my body, away from a screen, doing practical things and being in nature - being the natural creature that I am. The practical activities that I'm enjoying at the moment are growing vegetables, keeping goats and making clothes. I call this 'self-sufficiency'. I'm not entirely self-sufficient of course, but if all the aeroplanes stopped flying tomorrow and the supermarkets shut, I'd still have vegetables, dairy products, goat meat and clothes, straight off, before any local trading had started.

I call this a 'blended lifestyle,' in which you spend part of your work time doing traded work for money, and part of your work time doing practical work for you, your family or your friends. It's a blend of self-sufficiency and trade, one hand on the laptop, one hand on the spade.

In your version, your hands might be on different things. 'One hand on the stethoscope, one hand on the hammer,' for example, for a doctor who likes to build things. What would yours be?

THE SYSTEMIC POSSIBILITY

Lots of people seem to want something like a blended lifestyle.[1] And a lot of us would like to live in the country.[2] So what stops us?

In the beginning of the 19th century 10% of people in Britain lived in cities. 100 years later, 80% of us do.[3] We left the land - some by choice, others by force - in order to participate in the growing industrial economy. The land available for us to live and farm on was intentionally reduced, so that we would turn from self-sufficiency to wage labour in order to survive.

"If... every native is to be a landholder of a sufficient area on which to establish himself, then the question of obtaining a satisfactory labour supply will never be settled."

- Lord Delamere, Kenya, 1912[4]

---

[1] Or at least, most people I talk with. Also, 4 out of 10 UK adults under 35 dream of 'downshifting', according to research from the Prudential reported in 'Stress causes move to job downshifting', The Guardian, 15 October 2003.
[2] While 75% of Brits live in urban and suburban areas, 72% of people think they would be happier anywhere but a city, according to a Gallup poll. Even in 1963 61% of people wanted to live in rural areas but didn't. See 'London's comings and goings,' The Economist, August 2003.
[3] Rogers, Richard. Cities for a Small Country. F&F 2000
[4] McIntosh, Alastair: Soil and Soul, Aurum Press 2004:94

One hundred years prior, *"Lord and Lady Stafford were pleased humanely, to order a new arrangement of this Country. That the interior should be possessed by Cheviot [sheep] Shepherds and the people brought down to the coast and placed there in lots under the size of three arable acres, sufficient for the maintenance of an industrious family, but pinched enough to cause them turn their attention to the fishing [i.e. waged labour]."*

- Patrick Sellar, Lawyer, 1815[5]

The industrial economy created Patrick Sellar, Lord Delamere et al has brought us very useful wealth. It is now unsustainable.

But we cannot slow or reduce the economy, we believe, because people will lose their jobs and incomes. Without jobs and incomes, how will we meet our needs?

Fortunately, we are creative. So it it perfectly possible for us to re-imagine our ways of organising land and money, such that we can work for money part-time and be self-sufficient part-time at the personal or community level. That way, total employment can stabilise or reduce with wellbeing at least maintained, and probably enhanced.

---

[5] McIntosh, Alastair ibid.

Two hundred years ago it was thought that people would not want to move from local self-sufficiency to employment, so they had to be forced to, by reducing access to land.

Now, few people would altogether give up our jobs and put both hands on our spades. We like our incomes, our professional identities - some of us at least.

So we need not fear that by increasing opportunities for self-sufficiency we would reduce the available workforce. Rather we could reduce the *necessary* workforce and enable the economy to explore what "sustainable growth" means in practice.

By taking parts of our lives away from the money economy, we give it a bit of a breather, and let it find its next, unprecedented form.

So, A Manifesto....

I've never written a manifesto before. I'm not in a political party. I'm not creating one. Here's what I'm trying to do.

I'm trying to develop a lifestyle that makes sense at this time. A lifestyle that feels good.

I'm telling other people about it. When I do, they say they want it too, often, or something similar. But they say, it's not possible for everyone, just for a privileged few.

I've thought about that a lot. This lifestyle could be possible for many people, I've figured, if many people wanted it. But some things would need to change.

I've come to the conclusion that the lifestyle I'm trying to develop could be called a 'Post-Capitalist' lifestyle. It's difficult because we live in a Capitalist system.

If lots of people wanted to live a Post-Capitalist lifestyle, we could do it, but we'd need to develop a Post-Capitalist system.

So, I thought I'd clear a little time and try to lay out, as clearly as I can, what that might look like. This isn't an Anti-Capitalist text. I see Anti-Capitalism as a critical, divisive argument, and Post-Capitalism by contrast as a creative,

16

collaborative conversation.

'Capitalism' doesn't seem to be a single fixed thing. Some people say the essential characteristic is private ownership of the means of production. For others it's the use of money to make money, or profit as the primary motivation for enterprise. People describe differing varieties and forms of capitalism.

Here I'm going to treat Capitalism as an ideology, a set of ideas that underpins the dominant social and economic order. I describe it in 'Capitalism and Post-Capitalism on a post-card' on page 23.

By 'Post-Capitalism' I don't mean Socialism, Marxism or Communism; I don't mean a fixed vision or ideology, but rather the term under which we can converse about what set of ideas and values we might want to base our progress upon now, and what, then, that progress might look like.

I'm trying to talk to a few different people at once. I'm trying to talk to people who live lives. A lot of us yearn for things that somehow we don't think we can say, 'I want this. I want it to become real.' So to these people, I suppose I want to say, it's ok to ask for what you really want. And then ask: How do you want to live?

Some people have influence over things beyond their own lives.

In my totally ideal, my-thoughts-go-places-Mwahahah scenario, this piece would also talk to:

- People in the media and politics, so that Post-Capitalism enters public discourse as a legitimate thing to be speaking about, and that the debate opens doors into new possibilities for society

- Business people, to the end that we move away from the limited company model of ownership and towards even better models of ownership and finance, models that make sense at this time

- Policymakers who influence urban and rural planning, so that we do more blending of agriculture and the creative knowledge economy in urban and rural areas

- People in organisations, to create awareness and debate of the blended possibility as opposed to polarized boom or bust economic scenarios.

That's quite ambitious isn't it. OK well let's start and see where we get.

Capitalism Rocks

Capitalism is fantastic. Thanks to it, we have washing machines, modern dentistry, Skype and anesthetic. Women have the opportunity to be more than their husbands' housekeepers and PAs, a tiny likelihood of dying in childbirth, and very great likelihood that any children they bear will live long and prosper, sort of. We have safe streets (pretty much, in the UK at least), central heating, Goretex, great mountaineering equipment, excellent bicycles and fruit in winter.

Capitalism, We Thank You.

At the heart of Capitalism's genius is the way that it incentivises investment, creating an abundance of cash for innovation, in other words, the doing of New Stuff.

This crucial incentive creates a decentralized, agile market. Without it someone with a good idea would probably have to petition the government for startup money, or simply sit sadly on the idea while tending the cattle.

If enterprise and innovation are not supported, you end up with an economy based on agriculture, public services and charitable donation, and how can such a community ever propel itself?

Thanks to incentives to invest in innovation, we

have iPhones, inhalers and good contraceptives; we have work and we have wealth. This is baby and not bathwater, and - in thinking about the progression into Post-Capitalism, where we are of Capitalism and from Capitalism, taking some of its best features with us into the future - let's get clear on which we think is which.

CAPITALISM SUCKS

Is this the end of the story, or can we do better than this?

To really, properly shift up a level, we need a frank, profound, creative conversation about ideology.

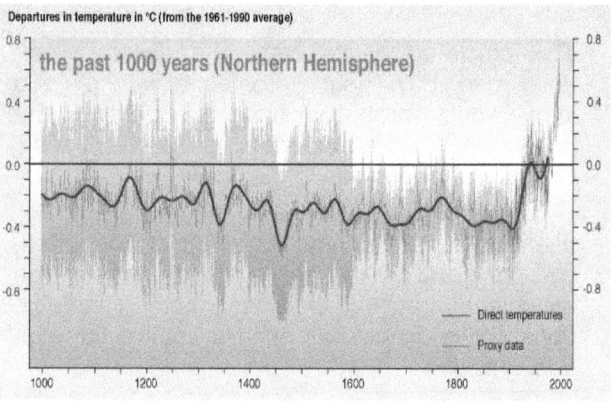

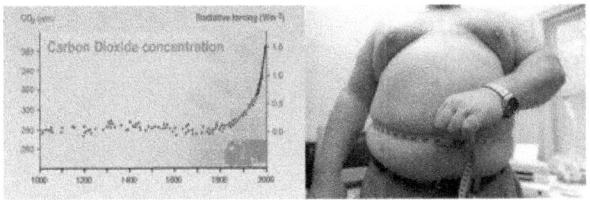

Carbon Dioxide concentration

CO_2 (ppm)   Radiative forcing (Wm⁻²)

From *The Times*

February 14, 2007

Britain's children are unhappiest in the Western world

Alexandra Blair, Education Correspondent

Stress Reduction Kit

Bang
Head
Here

Directions:
1. Place kit on FIRM surface.
2. Follow directions in circle of kit.
3. Repeat step 2 as necessary, or until unconscious.
4. If unconscious, cease stress reduction activity.

ACTUAL
Distribution of
Wealth in the U.S.

40%

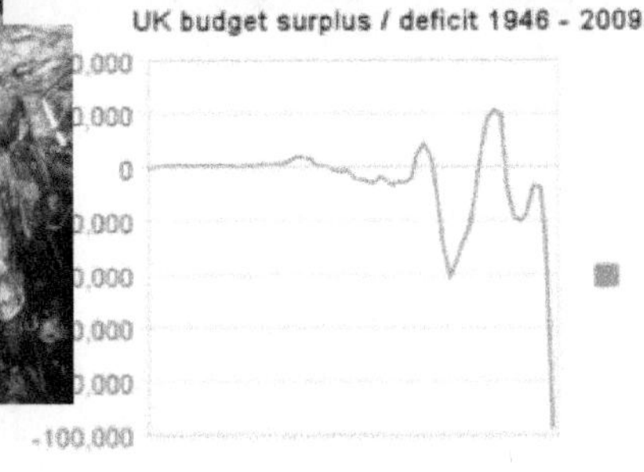

UK budget surplus / deficit 1946 - 2009

0

-100,000

CAPITALISM AND POST-CAPITALISM ON A POSTCARD

My take on this is pretty simple. I see Capitalist ideology as a set of value propositions that run like this:

- Wealth over well-being
- The head over the body and the heart
- Man over woman
- Science over nature
- God / non-God over spirit
- Control over chaos
- The individual over the collective.

My version of Post-Capitalism, then, is something that simply makes some tiny shifts:

- Wealth beside well-being
- The head beside the body, beside the heart
- Man beside woman
- Science beside nature
- God / non-God beside spirit
- Control beside chaos
- The individual beside the collective.

Manifesting it involves a re-imagining of almost everything.

It's worth saying that Post-Capitalism is happening a lot already. Everything covered in this manifesto has a complexity and evolution beyond the scope of this short text, and the Post-Capitalist possibilities I've laid out hope to be springboards for the imagination rather than final drafted visions.

I'm going to try to sketch out an overview, one thing at a time. Read it in any order you please.

I start with business because models of business finance are at the very heart of Capitalism and Post-Capitalism. Then work, because a new approach to work is at the heart of a Post-Capitalist lifestyle.

Then land, because new approaches to work potentially lead to new ways of organizing land. Next is family, because all of the above potentially change our experiences of family profoundly.

Then I play more loosely with other ideas around the body, politics, religion and joy.

Enjoy! Over to you. I hope you enjoy agreeing, disagreeing, and sitting back and imagining what you're going to do with the interesting situation we find ourselves in at the dawn of the twenty-first century.

PART TWO

CAPITALIST FORMS AND POST-CAPITALIST POSSIBILITIES

Business

Capitalist businesses are owned by distant shareholders and aim firstly to create wealth for those shareholders by maximising profits. This supports innovation and creates wealth, yet at the same time creates an unsustainable growth imperative, materialist consumer culture, and sharp wealth inequalities.

Post-Capitalist businesses aim firstly to make a useful contribution, and have no owners with a solely financial interest in them. This ultimately reduces the cost of living, inequality, the need for advertising, fast growth and stress at work. Things stay productive and interesting, while everything gets healthier.

CAPITALIST BUSINESS

Approaches to financing business are at the very heart of Capitalism as it is now, and Post-Capitalism as it could be. It may well be true that all else flows from here. Here's how:

1. People want to do New Stuff because we are inherently curious, creative and evolving. Typically we create new projects or organizations with which to do it. Great.

2. Doing New Stuff takes start-up finance. If entrepreneurs don't have it already, they must find it from somewhere.

3. There are many entrepreneurs all looking for investment. To compete, entrepreneurs offer potential investors the highest possible returns.

4. The entrepreneur who successfully secures investment must then find ways to continually create high profits in order to deliver the promised returns to the investor.

5. Profit and growth become the core aim of the business strategy. Sales must always rise. Costs must be minimized, prices maximized. Here begin the problems.

Some of the resulting dynamics are well known and widely criticized. For example:

*   The growth-oriented business must advertise as much as possible to increase

sales, spreading a materialist consumer culture.

- Consumer culture leads us to produce and consume ever more: forests fall, seas fill with plastic, and our carbon emissions continue to rise. We know that this approach to consumption and production is not sustainable.

- The effort to maximize margins and keep costs down can encourage companies to externalize the social and environmental costs of production. In other words, communities and nature pick up some of the downsides of the business activity and the cost of protection or repair is not included in the end price.

- Share-price emphasis can create unpleasant working environments.[6]

Further dynamics are less well understood. In particular, the impact of the plc model of ownership on wealth inequality is poorly understood. Raising this issue tends to provoke accusations of Communist leanings. I hope it's clear that to me, Post-Capitalism is not Socialism,

---

[6] Two useful texts explore this in some detail: Marjorie Kelly and Alan White's paper Corporate Design: The Missing Business and Public Policy Issue of Our Time. Boston, Tellus Institute, 2007, and Tomorrow's Owners: Stewardship of Tomorrow's Company. London, Tomorrow's Company, 2008.

Marxism or Communism. But this dynamic is important.

COMPANY OWNERSHIP AND THE DISTRIBUTION OF WEALTH

A Public Limited Company - or 'plc' for short ('publicly traded company' in the US) - can be thought of as a little piece of engineering, a kind of system or machine.

It takes *inputs* that include time from its employees and money from its customers.

It creates *outputs*, which include financial returns to shareholders.

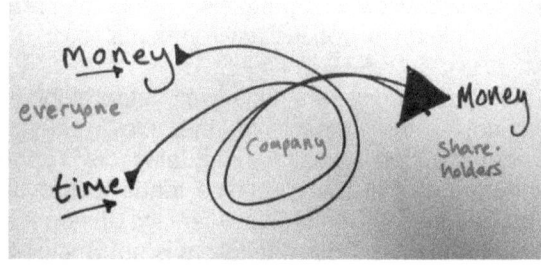

There are many employees and customers, some rich, some poor. Shareholders tend to be fewer, and richer. The more they own, the more they get - so wealth accrues with the wealthiest. It's a 'hoover up' effect, which is probably how America ended up with a wealth distribution that looks like this:

(The graph looks a bit strange because the wealth of the top 10% doesn't fit on it unless it's broken into pieces. The top 1% has 40% of the wealth, and so has a whole column to itself on, ironically, the far right.)

This most dominant of business models, then – the public limited or publicly traded company - acts as a mechanism that takes capital (money and time) from the many customers and employees, and channels it towards the few owners, creating wealth inequality. In the absence of strongly progressive taxation, this inequality becomes the extreme wealth inequality we see today.

---

[7] Wealth Distribution in the USA by TheRules.org at www.youtube.com/watch?v=rMhvYeQPOcE

A study by the Institute of Fiscal Studies found that the Stock Market in the US had a bigger impact on wealth inequalities than income, inheritance and education policies.[8]

Under Capitalist ideology, this is fine because wealth is more important than wellbeing and the individual is more important than the collective. This is how money is made and the "rising tide raises all ships". No problem. (This is commonly argued, despite the above chart clearly telling the story of a 'hoover-up' effect lifting a few ships and lowering the rest, rather than a shared benefit 'trickle down' effect in operation.)

WHAT THIS COULD MEAN FOR HOW WE LIVE

It almost goes without saying that employee time is our time. Consumer money is our money, which used to be our time before we traded it for money. The impact of the profit-maximising business model is that it costs more money and takes more of our time than other business models do.

Here's an example. I once lived in a student housing co-op in California. Our living costs were 66% of what our peers in private accommodation

---

[8] Banks, James et al (2000). *Wealth Inequality in the United States and Great Britain.* UK, Institute for Fiscal Studies and University College, London.

paid, primarily because profit was not being made from our housing and a lot of our food.[9] Living costs that are 1/3 lower make a big difference as a student to the time you can spend on earning, learning, projects, rest, play and love.

A mortgage provides a starker example. If you buy a home for £200k, take a 30 year mortgage at 4.3% and repay £1100 a month, after 30 years you will have paid £133k for the home and £188k in interest.[10] Your interest payments probably amount to several years of full-time work. If your mortgage is with a bank, a lot of your money (once your time) is becoming shareholder wealth via this mechanism. HSBC, for example, reported pre-tax profits of $22.1bn in 2007, much of which was gathered through mortgage interest and passed to shareholders.[11]

If dominant models of business ownership and finance were different, not only might we see more sustainable patterns of production and consumption; not only more power to the people within a company rather than outsiders with only a financial interest in what it does – but crucially, we may well also experience that life is cheaper and that we need to spend less time at work and

---

[9] Stokley, Jan. 'A legacy of Cooperative Studentship Yields Rich Rewards.' Berkeley Student Coop Newsletter' 08.

[10] My calculations.

[11] Kollewe, Julia. 'Record profits at HSBC'. The Guardian, March 5th 2007.

more time doing Other Things.

The lack of time currently available for Other Things like rest, play and love may be a big cause of stress, ill physical and mental health, family breakdown and unhappy children. Under Capitalist values, that's a shame but it is tolerated because the setup creates wealth, and wealth is more important than wellbeing.

Do you read the situation this way? If so, are you happy with it?

POST-CAPITALIST BUSINESS

We know that we need to amass surplus cash for New Stuff, otherwise we stagnate. We know that investment needs incentives otherwise it dries up. And I believe that the government should not be the primary source of start-up finance, because that becomes horribly centralized and bureaucratic.

So what do we do?

Recognising that this debate spans well beyond scope of this manifesto, I have five core points to emphasise.

1. THE PARTICIPATION PRINCIPLE

The plc model enables people who are only interested in an organisation's financial performance to have significant influence over its activity. Post-Capitalist business finance has a participation principle, meaning that investors must participate in the project in a way that is beyond putting up money and awaiting the return.

It may also open opportunities for micro-investment to a variety of stakeholders, all of whom have a relationship with the project that is about more than the money. An investment relationship that is just about the money doesn't work any more than a romantic relationship that is just about the sex. There has to be some heart in it.

2. FOURFOLD PURPOSE

Whereas Capitalist business aims to make a) profit and b) products and/ or services, Post-Capitalist businesses have a fourfold purpose:

- Make a useful contribution through the product or service(s). (For example, providing carpets to people who need carpets is a useful contribution.)

- Be financially sustainable. This involves making ends meet plus gathering surplus for rainy days, roof fixing and New Stuff.

- Internalise the full social and environmental costs of production.

- Look after your people.

Marjorie Kelly of Corporation 20/20 calls such a company a "for benefit" company: it may make profit, but social benefit is its ultimate purpose, not profit.[12]

---

[12] Kelly, Marjorie. 'Not just for profit.' Strategy+business issue 54, Spring 2009.

3. GOOD RETURNS

If wellbeing is as important as wealth and nature is as important as science, in economic terms this means that projects should be aiming to create social, economic and environmental capital in equal measure. In this case, typical economic returns will not be as high as they are in our current situation, where social and natural capital are compromised in order to create financial capital.

The mechanics of manifesting that in a competitive investment context are challenging, but may come down in part to lifestyles in which wellbeing is less dependent on money, and in which sharp wealth accumulation, as a result, is widely recognized as an unfulfilling goal – something that many investors already discover through experience.

4. STAKEHOLDER OWNERSHIP

I'm not sure this works for every project, but it works on paper for one I'm developing. We start with one or two owners (who have a relationship with the project that's not just about the money). They own 100% of the shares between them. As the project grows and stakeholders come in, they gradually buy shares from the primary owners, rather than just buying a service from them. It's as if rather than renting a flat, you gradually buy some of the flat from the landlord each month and when the flat is sold, you and the landlord and the other tenants share the gain accordingly. This is favourable if the collective is as important as the individual and wellbeing is as important as wealth. Stakeholder ownership and governance needs to be well-managed, of course, but if it is, it can produce some great outcomes.[13]

5. PENSIONS

Government used to pay pensions by collecting tax and giving some of it directly to pensioners. Now the British ratio of pensioners to working people is very high, so state pensions act more like private pensions, investing money and using stock market growth to deliver pension wealth. This isn't ideal because it relies on the stock market, which is volatile and arguably unsustainable.

How about land as a more (ahem) grounded alternative? Right now, "69 per cent of the acreage of Britain is owned by 0.6 per cent of the population", according to the New Statesman.[14] That isn't ideal if the collective is as important as the individual. Land-based pension schemes could broaden the distribution of land ownership.

---

[13] See, for example, Elinor Ostrom's 'Managing the Commons' for case studies. UK, Cambridge University Press, 1990.

[14] Cowley, Jason. 'Property Scandal.' New Statesman, 20 September 2004.

With your monthly pension payments, you gradually buy a piece of land. When you get old, you gradually sell your land to a youngster who is in turn stocking up for their old age. The income is your pension. It goes on ad infinitum. I can't work out the mathematics of whether it would keep you in hobnobs, but it's worth a think.

So. These five pillars of post-capitalist business...

1. The participation principle
2. Fourfold purpose
3. Good returns
4. Stakeholder ownership
5. Land-based pensions

...may help us to foster Post-Capitalist business activity that nourishes wealth and wellbeing, the individual and the collective, science and nature.

Different investment models may reduce the cost of living because a premium is not added to prices in order to satisfy shareholders. This could free up a lot of our time for The Good Life. Softening the need for growth and advertising could contribute massively to the emergence of a more sustainable context in which to play out our lives.

This may be why Frank Riboud, the CEO of Groupe Danone, says:

"I'm deeply convinced that [humanity's] future relies on our ability to explore and invent new business models and new types of business corporations."[15]

Frank thinks that *humanity's future* relies on *better business models.* (I have to say I largely agree. which is why I've put business first.)

How do you see it? What should we do? What would you do? What will you do?

---

[15] Quoted in Marjorie Kelly, 'Not just for profit.' Strategy+business issue 54, Spring 2009.

WORK

Capitalist work involves as much time and money as possible. Post-Capitalist work blends part-time work for money with part time practical, self-sufficient work and is more closely tailored to the specific gifts of the individual.

CAPITALIST WORK

The main purpose of working is to earn money. People aim to work and earn as much as they can because money is the key to getting what you need, from the right appearance to attract your mate to the coffin to bury you in.

Work is traded. We develop our skills and trade our time for money. We use money to meet our needs by trading with other people commercially.

The Capitalist employer must be primarily interested in employees' ability to generate value. This is because legally, her first priority must be to maximize shareholder profit, making wealth generation the imperative that everything else serves.

Work in Europe is positioned within a global work hierarchy. Western countries foster creative and knowledge economies. Eastern countries focus on services with some manufacturing, while Southern countries mix manufacturing with primary production. Western policy makers, anxious to retain competitive advantage, actively encourage this.

Education schools the individual into contributing to the needs of the dominant wealth creation mechanism.

Work is tiring. Energy is maintained with tea and biscuits. Personal consumption of edible oils rose 632% between 1966 and 1996 in the UK.[16] Producing this much oil is screwing the planet.[17] Ultimately this way of meeting our need for energy, pleasure and distraction reduces our overall energy and over time, it tends to make looking in the mirror an uncomfortable experience.

POST-CAPITALIST WORK

Individuals, families and communities meet our needs through a blend of self-sufficiency and trade. Many professionals like their work but find five days a week excessive, so time spent growing, building or making things is valued because the body and heart are as important as the head and practical work offers exercise to the body, time to the heart and peace to the mind.

Offices are located beside food gardens and teams do practical work together when they need to have conversations broader, deeper or more creative than the office tends to hold. People pop out for gardening breaks when they need a

---

[16] Consumption of Selected Household Foods, 1942 – 1996. UK National Food Survey, Food Statistics Branch, 2000.

[17] See, e.g., the noise about palm oil, the UK's most imported edible oil (Oil World Annual 2007, ISTA Mielke GmbH, Hamburg, Germany.)

breather from the intensity of office and screen, and a little time for just the right idea to bubble up while they're tending to the onions.

The blending of self-sufficiency and trade enables economic growth to slow safely. Because we find more of our needs are met through non-monetary activities and exchanges, we can reduce the time we spend working and earning. The increase in part time and flexible work enables organizations to slow down sanely.

Work is now based on motivation, trust and outcomes, and even love, identity and purpose. Work is contribution; even service. We each understand our purpose and contribute to it through work that is appropriate to our talents. This feels good.

Education is designed to identify and support the development of our individual leanings. Education is truly personalized, because wellbeing is as important as wealth; knowing your purpose, and serving it with appropriate work, is a core aspect of wellbeing.

Globally, each country has its doctors, brand strategists and farmers. No country is forced into forcing its people into its position in the top, middle or bottom of a global hierarchy.

LAND

Capitalist land is organized into urban and rural: large cities where people work, and broad countryside where big companies farm. Post-Capitalism by contrast draws lines around beautiful countryside we want to protect, and messes the rest up. Homes and communities become beautiful again, lots of people do a little bit of farming, and The Village emerges as the key concept for 21st century communities in cities and countryside alike.

Capitalist Land

Land is organized into urban and rural. Most people live in cities, where they work in organisations and meet most of their needs through paid-for goods and services, from food and shelter to personal development and childcare. This is great because it creates wealth: jobs, profits (that finance further economic activity) and taxes.

Within and between cities, most people travel by cars while a few people use public transport. Cars are preferred because they create personal freedom and wealth. Cars bring the government tax revenues, while trains cost the government tax expenditure. The frustration, death, pollution and illness created are sad but tolerated because wealth is more important than wellbeing and the individual is more important than the collective.

The countryside is mainly used for large-scale agricultural production, thought by some to be the most efficient way of farming, with some recreation and leisure use. Some people live in towns which are generally less exciting and wealthy than cities, but more peaceful.

In the beginning of the 19th Century, 10% of people lived in cities. By its end, 90% of people did.[18] 72% of us would rather live in the

---

[18] Rogers, Richard. Cities for a Small

countryside, MORI found, but we don't, because our jobs and friends are in the city now.[19]

POST-CAPITALIST LAND

The city enters the countryside and vice versa, while large stretches of wild, beautiful land remain protected from development.

Because professional management is based on trust rather than surveillance, and because of technologies that support communication across distance, teams no longer need to work in the same space all the time. People don't need to be in the city five days a week, so they move out. Local hub-like shared office spaces bubble up around the country and we work partly in our team office spaces in the city, and partly in the local shared offices. This reduces commuting. As more people move out of cities, rural Britain experiences social, professional and economic ebullience.

Barratt Homes is destroyed in a benevolent freak accident. New homes become beautiful again, and complementary to their environment, so that weekend walkers passing through a new village find it as pleasant as the open countryside

---

Country. F&F 2000

[19] Reported in 'London's comings and goings,' The Economist, August 2003.

they've just come from, rather like many villages that were built 200 years ago. This is continuity, even progress, rather than the regression in the aesthetic standards of most new buildings that we currently witness.

The demise of oil corresponds with a broad social yearning to get earth under the fingernails and hear the birds sing. The big pieces of agricultural land that characterized 20th century food production break into little pieces in urban and rural areas. People join in with food production if they want, and establish systems for participating and divvying up the goods. We produce and eat less wheat, which relies heavily on oil, and eat more nuts and fruits, which we can pick from the tree outside our window while we chat on the phone with a colleague about what to do about this or that.

City and national transport echo one another. Cities have a central network of fast, smooth, quiet, clean trams that whizz people, bicycles, buggies and baggage along the main arteries. Bicycles, agile little mini busses, and swipe-in, swipe-out general use cars fill the back streets. The almost entire removal of the car from cities frees up vast tracts of space for children, nature, allotments and pear trees. This happens because wellbeing is as important as wealth, nature is as important as science, and the collective is as important as the individual.

Nationally, a network of fast trains criss-crosses the country, which you swipe onto and off-of like you use an Oyster card on the London tube. A national car-share scheme and agile mini-busses create mobility for the last ten miles or so of your journey, which is where we really need the flexibility. The transport challenge of the 21st century - that cars are our main form of transport and yet create almost 25% of our CO_2 emissions - has been responded to with bold system-level innovation of the first order.

THE FAMILY

The economic context requires that Capitalist parents both work as near as possible to full time. Post-Capitalist parents tend to both work part time because of changes to business, work, and as a consequence, money. Things are owned and done privately in the Capitalist family, which tends to break down. The Post-Capitalist family is more rooted in the village, shares more, and has more time for love.

The Capitalist Family

The Capitalist family is private. It lives and parents privately. It owns washing machines, electric drills, juicers and gardens, privately. This is good for wealth because every family buys as many goods and services as possible.

Both parents work. This is because you can no longer raise a family on one income, in contrast to a generation ago. While house prices in the UK used to be broadly 3½ times *one* person's salary, they are now roughly 3½ times *two* people's salary, meaning that today's couple must put roughly ten days a week into traded work, compared to about half that just one generation ago.

Parenting, health, love, home, family, community, romance, rest and play are then squeezed into what little time is left after work. Many people feel rushed and stressed. Our children are reported to be the unhappiest in Europe.[20] Family life can be felt to be unbearable. As a result we are breaking up; marrying less and later, and divorcing more and sooner. Added to our longer life expectancy, this is pushing house prices yet higher, because the same number of people need more homes between us when we cannot get it and keep it together.

---

[20] Report Card 7: An overview of child wellbeing in rich countries. Italy, Unicef, 2007.

It's a vicious cycle, but it's ok because wealth is more important than wellbeing and every layer of this picture, from the extra work to the childcare, ready meals, extra homes and divorce lawyers - everything is good for GDP.

Children play with readymade games and technologies which define and constrain the creative territory of their play, thus limiting their learning, cognitive and creative development. That's ok because it doesn't take parental or community time and is good for business. We have become rich, poor and loveless, all at the same time.

THE POST-CAPITALIST FAMILY

Closer community (enabled by the time freed up from work by the blended lifestyle and Post-Capitalist models of business finance) enables more things to be shared, from power tools to childcare. We expect our partners to meet fewer of our needs, which are met through a variety of roles and relationships. Because there is more time in life, there is more time for love. Relationships are generally good.

Because economic capital is as important as natural and social capital, and because surpluses are not maximized, our money goes further as less goes to distant shareholders. Time and money are more evenly distributed around the population. In other words, our inequality is far less extreme.

A couple trades about 5 days a week between their collective potential of 14 days. This is shared between the parents; part time and flexible work is normal among both males and females. Contribution to home, family and community is recognized as equally valuable to traded economic contribution, because wellbeing is as important as wealth, women are as important as men, and the collective is as important as the individual.

The concept of the village re-emerges in the 21st century: the urban village, the rural village. Rural villages are connected through movement and technology to the social, professional and cultural opportunities of the city; urban villages are community-strong within high density, thriving cities, empty of the ugly roar of traffic and full of pear trees and kids' games where the cars of the old days used to be parked.

THE BODY

The Capitalist body runs on toxic stimulants provided by the capitalist matrix in order to maximise compliance and productivity within that matrix. The post-capitalist body runs on natural energy to follow natural instincts and thus it does good, looks good, and feels good from the inside.

THE CAPITALIST BODY

The Capitalist body mediates experiences through substances consumed. Caffeine to wake up in the morning; sugar and more caffeine to stay up during the afternoon lull; alcohol to unwind in the evening and particularly at the weekend, to unwind from the tension created by the caffeine and sugar, and also from the restrictive effort of shaping oneself into unnatural roles. Cigarettes and occasionally other drugs can also be added to enhance or create an outflow for the intensities of highs and lows experienced.

Caffeine, sugar, alcohol and nicotine are all addictive, which is bad for wellbeing and good for wealth. While individuals, families and communities battle to a greater or lesser degree with their relationships with these substances, the companies providing them create wealth which is great for jobs and tax. Because they make money - Cadbury, for example, announced pre-tax profits of £559 million in 2008[21] - the substances are offered everywhere, so that in a given day an individual will experience multiple opportunities to consume them, adding value to wealth and taking value from wellbeing.

The Capitalist body varies from anorexia to obesity. Food is anything but a simple source of

---

[21] http://uk.reuters.com/article/idUKLN62221320090225

nutrition. Significant energy and money is spent on trying to achieve the right body shape; this effort creates jobs and tax revenue. At the same time, the ever-present temptations of Capitalist food and lack of opportunities for physical activity pervert these intentions. Persistent anxieties are created; that's ok because wealth is more important than wellbeing.

Sleep and exercise are less important than work, so are taken when possible but compromised when work needs the time instead. This is because wealth is more important than wellbeing.

Exercise is taken in activities that are disassociated from a wider purpose, particularly in classes and at the gym.

Capitalist food has as many layers of post-production as possible. The more that raw ingredients can be combined, enhanced, packaged, transported, sold and marketed, the better because each layer of production creates another opportunity to create wealth. It's good also to involve science and industry in agriculture as much as possible. It doesn't matter if food produced is harmful to people or the environment, because science is more important than nature and wealth is more important than wellbeing.[22]

---

[22] Statistics from Sweden show a sharp increase in cancer rates after manufactured chemicals were introduced to

Because the head is more important than the body or the heart, Capitalist sex is led by the expectations and aims of the head more than by the instincts and feelings of the body and heart.

The male orgasm is more important than the female orgasm, and happens more often as a result. This is OK because men are more important than women. In pornographic representations of Capitalist sex, the female is usually at the service of male pleasure, rather than an experience of mutuality. Tradable artefacts such as sex toys, underwear, accessories and pornography are valued b \\\\\\\\ecause they contribute to wealth. Pornography, where the sex act is harnessed, controlled and manufactured into a tradable commodity, spreads ideas about sex and reinforces these norms.

The Capitalist body becomes ill, quite understandably. Illness is addressed by a National Sickness Service, which ignores the body in health and tends to it in sickness, providing medicines. In doing so, the service functions very effectively as a channel between the Capitalist body and pharmaceutical companies, which create great wealth by

---

agriculture in the 1950s. In the UK we don't have reliable cancer data prior to the 1970s so the relationship is less obvious. Around one third of people in Britain contract cancer in their lifetime, and about a quarter of us die from it.

providing for the sick. That is good because wealth is more important than wellbeing, and pharmaceutical companies create jobs, profits and tax revenues, which are important in a money-based society. The service is paid for by the public.

The Capitalist body dies, normally in hospital, and is mourned (briefly) at a funeral organized by a funeral company.

THE POST-CAPITALIST BODY

Tiredness is a sign of the body's need to rest; when tiredness is felt, therefore, rest is taken. This is ok because wellbeing is as important as wealth, and the body is as important as the head.

Addictive stimulants that are harmful to the body, primarily sugar, caffeine, alcohol and nicotine, are taken in moderation, but are not a regular part of life and any addiction or dependency is worked on until wholly removed. These stimulants are not used to hide mental or emotional discomfort. Rather, this discomfort is taken as a signal of something, and time is spent sitting in the discomfort until its nature and need are understood and responded to appropriately. As a result, the individual develops wisdom and this helps wellbeing.

The Post-Capitalist body eats foods in quantities

and frequencies that reflect the body's need. Exercise is often part of a broader story: a social story – dancing, long walks with a friend or partner; making love; playing high energy games and sports; practical activities like chopping wood or gardening; a spiritual practice that creates hormonal balance and an experience of mental peace, such as yoga.

The Post-Capitalist body in death is returned to the earth in the way that best feeds it. Full mourning takes as long as it needs.

Post-Capitalist sex is free of expectations or aims from the head; it is led by the feelings and instincts of the heart and the body. What it feels like is more important than what it looks like.

Post-Capitalist food is fresh, and local, and healthy, and seasonal, and made with love, eaten together, and really, really tasty.

From the inside, the Post-Capitalist body feels good.

Politics

Capitalist Politics

All political parties currently operate within Capitalism. Ideology is invisible and taboo. David Miliband says, "we must return to the growth that is essential in a modern industrial society."[23] Publicly, he takes for given the modern industrial society. If Miliband, one of our greatest political minds, is not publicly discussing ideology, then who is?

Money equals Power and well-paid corporate lobbyists have a greater influence over policy than any other stakeholder. Which is mostly why today's world, and our daily news, looks the way it does.

Post-Capitalist Politics

The role of politicians is to hold conversations about both the management of what is, actually, and the possibility of what might be, ideologically. Ideology returns as a discussion topic.
MPs become Talkaoke hosts and take their fun roundtable discussions out and around the place,

---

[23] Any Questions? Radio 4, 26th March 2010.

all the time, talking with everyone, talking in the streets, talking in the pubs, talking outside the school gates and the offices. Using our sophisticated technology we have lots of referendums, and these exciting big conversations enable people to make their decisions issue by issue. Politics becomes more accessible and manageable in the public mind; the wisdom of the crowd is fostered and trusted.

Voters are grouped into communities of place, as they currently are, and into non-spatial communities of interest. So you get one vote for being from Battersea, and one vote for being a conservative wildlife lover, or whatever you are. Currently more people are members of charities than political parties, but these values-based associations are largely divorced from democratic politics.

Campaign funding and political lobbying is somehow (answers, anyone?) so fair that it feels good in our *bones*.

We are more than consumers. We have minds. Politics is for people. In Post-Capitalism, we reorganize and reconnect.

RELIGION

CAPITALIST RELIGION

There is a man called God who does or does not exist.

God is mainly communed with via the head and sometimes the heart, but not really via the body. This is because the head is more important than the body and control is more important than chaos.

Religious communities do some very lovely things that bring communities together, weave good values into life, support the vulnerable, and mark the passage of time with different flavours. But your neighbour who doesn't share your faith can't come.

Jesus was a dude who had some wise things to say that still hold sway in our time. Eve unfortunately was a bit of a fuckup, (apple biting and all that), so ladies, sorry, you come second now. Once priestesses, now sandwich makers and flower arrangers.

Heaven and Hell are places you go after death that no-one can prove or disprove. If you don't want to suffer you have to obey the religious leaders' definition of what sends you where. That puts you sort of in their control. That's ok because control is more important than chaos.

POST-CAPITALIST RELIGION

Publicly or secretly, most people like giving it up to a higher power of some sort. Sacred spaces call us into our better selves and humble us softly. This is good. Sacred spaces abound. They are accessible community spaces where values are discussed and woven into daily life, the vulnerable are supported and the passage of time is marked with different flavours, themes and celebrations.

Jesus was a Dude who said some wise stuff that is still relevant today. Like lots of people. We learn from many in our personal and spiritual development.

The heart and body are as important as the head, so activities that make us feel connected to 'spirit' or a 'higher power' through the head, the body and the heart become fairly normal.

Some people and groups organize their relationship to spirit through a religion. That's fine. Others don't. That's fine too. No-one is going to go to hell if they don't do what you say, unless you really want to believe that.

This is all because spirit is as important as god /not god, chaos is as important as control, the

63

body and heart are as important as the head, the collective is as important as the individual, woman is as important as man, and wellbeing – of which personal development and reflection is obviously part – is as important as wealth.

All of the Post-Capitalist values are reflected in our spiritual lives.

JOY

CAPITALIST JOY

Joy is usually to be found with friends and loved ones. After that, it's like this.

Joy is generally found through entertainment, culture, and the pub.

Entertainment is consumed. Beer. Cinema. Television. Computer Games. Theatre tickets. Artists broadcast to a passive, paying audience. We are cultural consumers, consumers of joy. Instead of picking up an instrument or breaking into song, we press play.

Within the limited bounds of acceptable public behaviour we cannot really emote, so we sedate. Alcohol is good because it creates a lot of wealth, from breweries and vineyards to pubs and the companies that own half our pubs.[24] As a whole the industry makes up 2% of UK GDP.[25]

The broadcast model of culture - where the professional artist performs for a large, passive audience - is great, particularly when the ratio of culture consumers to culture producers is very high, because that generates more wealth.

Culture fragments, so little is shared among different ages, classes and ethnicities. We can't all sing the same songs any more, but that's ok because the individual is more important than the collective and commercial music creates more wealth than social music. Social music is difficult to turn into a commodity, so it is culturally peripheral.

Children are offered DVDs and computer games that reduce the scope of their play and thus their opportunity for intellectual, emotional and creative development.[26] Also it's sedentary so

---

[24] Pub companies owned 53% of UK pubs in 2007, according to the *UK Public Houses Market Development report* from Market & Business Development. The Wellington Pub Company, for example, owns 850 UK pubs. It is owned in turn by the Ruben Brothers, a private company. Forbes Magazine's *List of billionaires 2010* ranked David and Simon Ruben as second in the richest people in the UK, according to Wikipedia. http://en.wikipedia.org/wiki/David_and_Simon_Reuben

[25] Oxford Economics: 'The economic outlook for the UK drinks sector…' February 2009.

they get fat. That's ok because wealth is more important than wellbeing, and no-one has much time for anything else. Carry on.

POST-CAPITALIST JOY

We can make our own fun. Everyone has different play preferences, from the Musicians and the Jokers to the Kinaesthetes who like to move and be in their bodies, the Storytellers, the Artists, the Explorers and the Directors who bring people together and make it all happen.[27]

We know our play preferences and develop them for fun and for social contribution. We create participatory celebrations, and the Christmas song 'Tomorrow will be my dancing day' regains its meaning as seasonal dances return.

We get together in social spaces and have a drink from time to time but don't rely on alcohol for our freedom, our wildness, our disinhibition, our intimacy and our joy.[28]

Our practices of collective joy don't make much

---

[26] Brown, Stuart. 'Play'. US, Avery 2009

[27] Brown, ibid.

[28] For more on this, see Barbara Ehrenreich's wonderful book Dancing in the Streets: A History of Collective Joy. US, Granta Books, 2008.

money, don't emit much carbon, don't always make sense, and that doesn't matter at all. It's great fun.

Play makes love, between couples, families, communities, colleagues, friends and strangers.[29] Opportunities to play together, properly, purely, invigorate our souls, bring joy to our lives, and kindle love. Hurrah.

---

[29] US-based play and fitness specialist Frank Forencich reports that play stimulates oxytocin in the brain. Oxytocin is 'the love hormone,' associated with feelings of trust, intimacy and bonding. http://wildfitnessblog.com/

PART THREE

WRAPPING UP

Ten things that would be great now

1. Politics to reclaim ideology, and ideological diversity and debate, as its rightful territory. Let's explicitly talk about the ideological roots of our ills and the Post-Capitalist possibilities. The notion of Post-Capitalism to be debated and developed.

2. No new public limited companies to be floated. All new enterprises to become 'for benefit', companies as Marjorie Kelly calls them. Someone clever to figure out what to do with all the plcs that are already in existence.

3. A better term than 'for benefit' to be found, because it rings of state aid.

4. The relationship between dominant models of business ownership and the distribution of wealth to be freely debated and widely recognized.

5. The ideas of the Post-Capitalist / for benefit business to be debated and improved upon.

6. Dads of young children: go part time. Don't worry about the money. Don't worry about your organisation's culture. You'll change it. Go for it.

7. Everyone: move to the country if you want to. Make sure your home looks nice. Build it yourself if you want. Ask Viv Goodings if you need help, invite some friends and make a party of it.

8. Everyone: *only do what you love.* Stop doing things you don't love. You'll figure out how. Ask for part time or flexible working relationships if you want them. Pick up a spade if you want to. Reduce your dependency on the trade of your time, if you want to. Grow vegetables. Milk animals. Make furniture, buildings, clothes or toys for children. Give stuff away to your friends and neighbours. Everything you give will come back tenfold.

9. Department for Transport: Amazing system-level innovation in our transport system, please. Fast trains and trams, shared cars, pear trees.

10. Anyone who gets this far: try going to a ceilidh sometime. They're fun.

Capitalist and Post-Capitalist values in a little more detail

Wealth over Wellbeing

The roots of Capitalism can be seen in a variety of points in history. Whether it's 1800, 1500 or 2000 BC, we can be sure that when Capitalism emerged, many people were hungry and cold and dying from minor ills. So for our forefathers and mothers, wealth was genuinely a primary route to wellbeing.

Wealth beside Wellbeing

An absence of wealth can compromise wellbeing. But beyond a certain point, increases to wealth are found to make no difference to wellbeing.[30] As too much energy goes into wealth creation, wellbeing can be damaged. Post-Capitalism understands that wealth is but one facet of wellbeing and adjusts social and political priorities accordingly.

---

[30] See, for example, the 'Progress Paradox' widely discussed by Tim Jackson and the new economics foundation.

MAN OVER WOMAN

Men's work traditionally creates more financial wealth than women's work, so men are correspondingly valued more highly, with women playing a supportive, follower role.

MAN BESIDE WOMAN

Gosh don't know what to say here. It's just obvious innit?

THE HEAD OVER THE HEART AND THE BODY

The intelligence of the head is the primary engine of wealth creation. The body is the necessary servant of the head. The heart is the territory of values and sense of intrinsic purpose, which have to be put aside sometimes in order to get on with wealth creation. The heart can get in the way, so it is made less important.

THE HEAD BESIDE HEART, BESIDE BODY

The body and heart tell us important things, for our wellbeing, for our relationships, and for finding our ways forward in a complex life. Through valuing the body and heart, we help ourselves find love and peace. It's hippy vernacular, perhaps, but take these things away from your life and what are you left with?

SCIENCE OVER NATURE

Nature seemed infinite, and yet unpredictable and sometimes against us. Science is the way to tame nature and harness it for our advantage, particularly for wealth creation.

SCIENCE BESIDE NATURE

Science helps us do things we value, like cure sickness and communicate across distance. Ultimately, nature is more intelligent than we are. It is a wise parasite that respects its host.

CONTROL OVER CHAOS

How do you extract value from chaos? Chaos has its own ideas about what to do.

CONTROL BESIDE CHAOS

Or "chaorder" as Dee Hock calls it.[31] The most beautiful, potent and effective forms of order tend to emerge from well-managed chaos. A bit less trying and a bit more listening and letting can produce surprisingly magical result

---

[31] See, for example, Hock, Dee. One from Many: VISA and the rise of the Chaordic Organisation. Berrett-Koehler '05.

GOD / NON-GOD OVER SPIRIT

'Spirit' is a bit vague, isn't it? And for many is primarily intuited through the body and heart. As the head is dominant, a heady route to spirituality is needed; narratives of Gods provide this.

GOD / NON-GOD BESIDE SPIRIT

Spirituality tends to enrich our lives and social behaviour. Gods were, perhaps, always a mass-communication device for abstract concepts and social values. That can be helpful to some people. 'Spirit' is a more inclusive concept; everyone has their own idea about what it is and how to relate to it, and the acceptance of diversity helps to bring it into our personal and collective lives.

THE INDIVIDUAL OVER THE COLLECTIVE

Entrepreneurs and innovators are the primary spark of wealth creation. If the collective is prioritised, innovators are constrained because they think and do unconventional things. We must be able to compete, think and look out for ourselves in order to be most active in shopping, working and innovating.

THE INDIVIDUAL BESIDE THE COLLECTIVE

We like to be free. And we need each other. Healthy individuals make healthy communities. Healthy communities make healthy individuals. Ultimately, I think, Post-Capitalism is about the true health of everything.

THE END

Thank you for reading

Over to you.

Yours,

An optimist

London, May 2010